EVEN WHEN WE SLEEP

Books by Marilyn Kallet

How Our Bodies Learned (poetry)

The Love That Moves Me (poetry)

Disenchanted City, Chantal Bizzini (translation, with Brad Anderson and Darren Jackson)

The Big Game, Benjamin Péret (translation)

Packing Light: New and Selected Poems (poetry)

Last Love Poems of Paul Eluard (translation)

Circe, After Hours (poetry)

The Movable Nest: A Mother/Daughter Companion (with K.S. Byer)

Jack the Healing Cat

The Art of College Teaching: 28 Takes (with A. Morgan)

One For Each Night: Chanukah Tales and Recipes

Sleeping With One Eye Open: Women Writers and the Art of Survival (with J. O. Cofer)

How to Get Heat Without Fire (poetry)

Worlds in Our Words: Contemporary American Women Writers (with P. Clark)

A House of Gathering: Poets on May Sarton's Poetry

Honest Simplicity in William Carlos Williams's "Asphodel, That Greeny Flower"

In the Great Night (poetry)

Devils Live So Near (poetry)

EVEN WHEN WE SLEEP

Poetry by Marilyn Kallet

BLACK
WIDOW
PRESS

Boston

Joseph S. Phillips and Susan J. Wood, Ph.D., Publishers
www.blackwidowpress.com

Cover art: *Memory, Like Lace, Is Full of Holes*, Mindy Weisel, acrylic, gouache, oil pastel on handmade paper, Series 2020.
Author photo: Christophe Gardner
Design & production: Kerrie L. Kemperman

ISBN-13: 978-1-7371603-2-8

Printed in the United States
10 9 8 7 6 5 4 3 2 1

Acknowledgments

Thanks to my husband, Lou Gross, for inspiring my life and singing my poetry! Grateful that my daughter, Heather Hanselman, has a keen eye for copy. Glad that Elaine Zimmerman is both my sister and poetry sister. Fervent thanks to Joe Phillips, at Black Widow Press, for standing by his authors in difficult times. Kerrie Kemperman's graphic designs for Black Widow Press always lift our poetry.

All my thanks to U.S. Poet Laureate Joy Harjo, for showcasing "Beggar" as a "Poem-a-Day," Poets.org. On March 18, 2020, Yo-Yo Ma performed "Songs of Comfort" on PBS and encouraged others to compose them. Many poems in this collection were inspired by his call for daily songs. Daniel Lawless at *Plume,* Marianne Worthington at *Still,* and Katherine Smith at *Potomac Review* have given my work breathing room. Pamela Uschuk edited a needed issue of *Black Earth Institute* on "Dignity as an Endangered Species." Thanks to Matthew E. Silverman and Nancy Naomi Carlson, for *101 Jewish Poems for the Third Millennium;* to Katerina Stoykova at *Literary Accents;* Richard Krawiec and crew at *One;* and Keith Flynn at *Asheville Poetry Review.* Retiring *New Letters* editor, Robert Stewart, will be missed. Deborah Levine at *American Diversity Report* hosts vital cross-cultural conversations. Poets Deborah Harper Bono, Sean Purio, and Allison Pittini Davis provided insightful notes. Dr. Julia Demmin cheered me on and offered editing advice. Photographers Christophe Gardner, John Alexander, and Diane Fox gave suggestions about cover design. Mindy Weisel's painting, *Memory, Like Lace, Is Full of Holes,* covers the volume in brilliant blue, and I am grateful.

I'm thankful to Mayors Rogero and Kincannon and to the City of Knoxville for embracing my work and to Liza Zenni and Suzanne Cada at the Arts & Culture Alliance of Greater Knoxville for continued encouragement. My pre-pandemic time as Knoxville Poet Laureate was joyful. Grateful that Mayor Victor Ashe keeps my work in view. Thanks to my poetry sister, Rhea Carmon and to The Fifth Woman ensemble, for taking poetry to underserved sites in our city. Grateful to Knoxville Symphony Conductor Aram Demirjian for his lyrical visions. Thanks to Miriam Esther Wilhelm and the Stanford Eisenberg Knoxville Jewish Day School for inviting me to participate in the "Violins of Hope" programs; these concerts featured violins rescued from the Holocaust. Nashville musician/poet Matt Urmy recently showcased my poetry with his podcast. Thanks to Margaret Renkl at *The New York Times* and Maria Browning at Humanities Tennessee, for keeping Tennessee writers in the news. *Merci* to Cheryl Fortier and John Alexander at VCCA-France for halcyon days in Auvillar. *Merci* to the Brunes, the Dassonvilles, to Lucy Anderton *et famille* and to the Macallisters for good company, for keeping me well-fed and infused! *Merci* to Hotel Quartier Latin in Paris for "The Poet's Room."

Some of these poems have been published in journals and anthologies. Many thanks to the editors.

"You Can't," "Soft Song," *One*
"Even the Alchemists," *New Letters*
"Beggar," *Poets.org,* Academy of American Poets
"Nothing Good Can Come," *Literary Accents*
"Word Man," *Thrush*
"Entreaty," *Descant*
"The Mysteries," *Blue Fifth Review*
"Travelogue from the River of Lethe," *North American Review: Open Space*

"Comfort Song in a Time of Peril," *Black Earth Institute*

"Small Song," *Potomac Review*

"Breakfast in Paris," *Nashville Hip*

"Practicing," *SynoptiQ*

"Let the Phantoms Go," *Nouveau's Midnight Sun*

"Letters from Earth & Sky," *Plume*

"Ode to Ragweed," "Ode to My Lost Glove," *Still: The Journal*

"The Morels," "The Biggest Blue Jay," *American Diversity Report*

"Correspondences," *The Pigeon Parade Quarterly*

"Removed," *101 Jewish Poems for the Third Millennium*

"No One," *New Voices Project: Contemporary Writers Confronting the Holocaust*

"Violins of Hope, Knoxville," Knoxville Mayor's website; excerpt, *About Place Journal*

"Love Song to the Kind Ones," "Practicing," *Alte*

"No Egg, No Pony," *Backstory*

To Lou, always

Even When We Sleep

III. Sing the Unsung

IV. If Love Whispers

Même quand nous dormons nous veillons l'un sur l'autre...

Even when we sleep we watch over one another...

—Paul Eluard

I. Even The Alchemists

You Can't

My horoscope says, "You can't find love
by seeking it,

so go create
beauty."

Sure, would you like a side
of Aeolian harp strings with that?

Or a Grecian urn-chip
stamped with well-turned

men? "Are you done?"
the stars hummed.

"Weave lines like ivy
wrapping the sycamore,

slips that don't need
us, almost weightless,

like the crisp magnolia
leaf you keep near the dash

for company,
tan like Spanish leather,

like that boy in Seville (what
was his name?) Fifty years

back. I bet
he remembers."

Even The Alchemists

Even the alchemists started
with lead.

With you, I'd have to invent
the flask and dross.

When Neruda tasted *nada,*
he sighed, *Quiero.*

I want what I do not have.
From emptiness

he shaped blues
Coltrane

might have envied.
Start there.

Put on a *Love Supreme*
and wear it

like satin,
something

to cling to, that
clings back.

Starter kit:
Coltrane,

Neruda,
ache.

Do not
dilute.

Permission

In this one
small square of light
permit me, since
all else

is forbidden,
to sing to you.
Your poems lift
me to the

Rockies,
eagles'
view. How
sinewy the
rivers bend,

sinewy,

and like a
grade-school kid
I relearn the
power of words:

sin, you,
me.

Word Man

I understand Mary Shelley,
Frankenstein, the desire
to forge a man out of spare
parts, even if things go wrong.

My machinery is made of
words, I want you
here. Instead of an arm,
a line, it's what

we have. Babies
want.
Adults, too. We jam
the space of a page

with font, fancy
loops. Freud
knew. I bid you:
Come back, come

here. We pay
for charms
and voodoo,
shop for something,

anything. Over-
eat. Want you
here. In
my mouth.

Soft Song

Nothing about you is soft,
sir.

When people thank you for
your service

I wonder if
I am serviceable.

But this is a soft
song, a petal-wreath

that crowns you for being
funny, wise,

and yes,
tightly wired

with respect to
muscles.

Thank you for
humoring me

with songs.
With respect, sir,

words are all we offer.
As a young poet wrote,

"Let's be grateful
for what we can have."

1996, I shredded
that letter

with my teeth.

Beggar

Just one!
I begged the Muse.

You again?
Always the same

schtick.
If you want the line,

you'll have to earn it.
How?

Write about something
besides younger men,

Muse said.
Think of Elizabeth Bishop,

who spent twenty years
on "The Moose."

No! I won't!
Too late. I was already

minding my
mousse

au
chocolat.

Entreaty

This morning I whispered to you
through the soft mic
of a magnolia blossom.

Write to me, I said.
or I will be a ghost
of love, pale,

past my season.
Your words are
rain and

sun, night-blooming
stars, embodied.
Firm. Words

hold us.
Without them,
days taste the same.

Days
tumble over
each other, down

the gravel path.
Write to me.
Alas, no Paris

this spring.
I tour my backyard,
and irises just budding

wrap blatant
messages. The azaleas
are shedding deep

pink silk, all
one kind, unless
you break

the silences
with your tongue.

The Mysteries

(Meditation on "Cracked" by Bernard Heise)

The summer the Dome crashed Stephen King grew richer.
I didn't hear a thud when you went dark.
No hamburger half-cows littered the fence line.

Nada.
Tuli jumped off the Brooklyn Bridge
and lived. You leaped into the blank without a splash.

When I went out searching,
mud cracked into obscure maps.
I'll admit the breaks were breathtaking.

Maybe I'll also gleam with loss,
like those cracked Japanese cups sealed with
gold leaf.

Today there's tarnished copper underfoot.
Baked mud beckons like gingerbread.
Sidewalk cake

hints incarnation.
Who finds divine direction
in dirt?

As kids, we played witches with dousers.
Little *voyants* roamed up and down
the leafy dead-end on Vernon.

Cards in our bike spokes ticked.
We nestled pretty street rocks
in tins next to fifty-cent aggies.

The summer the Buddha left his father's palace
on PBS, I ate it up, fed
by his tears turned drinking water.

I'd forgotten you in the downpour.
Is that still me raining blues,
becoming seedbed, nimbus?

Is that you strumming Morrison's "The End"
behind the walls
of your ex-wife's house?

Travelogue from the River of Lethe

Your sign beckoned, *Step in,*
Beautiful.

I wanted to shed memories
like clothes

on a summer day,
to shed time,

not tears. My choice:
toe in.

I remembered your face,
wiry body,

your lure. You insisted
I was beautiful.

One toe, I told myself.
I remembered that Galway

spoke of a hard time
finding the path through the forest

toward the end, that Bly
read everything twice.

I remembered your beauty, though
the river promised no regrets.

You were there, fishing for the forgetful.
This time, I didn't bite.

Spiritual

What power has love during
a pandemic?

Ours was always
virtual.

Plato called it.
Kind love

swells,
stronger,

like a muscle
that has been working

out, but lighter,
invisible,

like atomic
weights—

love that lifts us
daily without

hope of
gain.

We practiced
for this.

Virtual, virtuous,
faute de mieux.

Write to me,
Buddy.

Plato, play dough.
Mixed metaphors

taste good.
Honey, words

are all we have
& hold.

Comfort Song in a Time of Peril
(March 18, 2020)

Sleep, little one,
Mama has washed her hands.
Daddy won't touch his face

again. We will keep you
from harm
with love and antibacterial

wipes. We'll scrub
everything twice.
Mommy will keep Daddy happy

with her tongue. Wait,
that's a different poem!
Mommy will sing you a

powerful, germ-free lullaby.
Sleep, little one,
Trump's an idiot,

but you will grow up
to be smart,
empowered,

fearless.
And by then
there will be a vaccine

and a Democrat.

What I Do When I'm Afraid

Write poems to you,
of course. Though today,
at the doctor's office,
I didn't have pen
or pad, so I bled
my rough draft
into a tube.

Hope you won't be
peeved. The scare
was real. And
love? Like you said,
"a secret lake," greater
than fear, than the
skin, the
body.

Housebound

"If a mouse slipped in
I would name him

Merlin," Lou said.
My hub's not a poet,

but he knows
the power

of names. He's my
mage, my wand,

my weaver
of spells. He would

also be my agent,
if poetry

made money.
For now, he'll fry

matzo brei and
clean up, indulge me

in naming ants
and gently

placing them
one by one

on the lawn.
Melvin, have a sweet life.

Madison, keep your
legs on. Do ants

have tongues?
Lou would know.

He's literate and
numerate. He does our taxes

and calls me pet names,
names you would

never
call a mouse.

Cranky Birds

I tossed egg matzo
crumbs and the blue jays
threw shade.

What?
You wanted
brioche?

Soon, I'll fling
some
leavened bits.

Then the biggest one
snatched the
biggest crumb

& flew it to
the neighbor's
greener

lawn.
"See?
Ever heard

of delivery?
Get with
the program!"

Jay, when I was
small, delivery
did not exist.

"No?
Then how did
You get here,

smart mouth?"
You're right.
That nice

Dr. Monsky
in Montgomery
delivered.

Two a.m., he
worked his gloved
magic

on my
etherized
ma.

Knock me
out again,
if we

don't get
out of this house
soon!

Deliver me!
"O stop," the jays
tweeted.

"Halt the
drama! Go for
yer stupid

half-inch run,
then ring
the nearest deli!"

Apology, to Lou

Sorry for yelling
when I spilled the coffee.
Sorry for stains on the rug

that resemble squalling babies.
Sorry for grey rain
that nails us.

Sorry for not trusting
that you would heed
my cry.

Sorry we rewatched
a half hour of "The Marriage."
Adam Driver's dynamite,

nu? Ferris Bueller
offered the cure.
Sorry made of coffee grounds

and mean rain.
Sorry made of wet grass
and heat rash.

Sorry made of I'll leave you
the last brownie
and Ritter Sport Dark

that will arrive in Some Day's mail.
Sorry made of cheap
toilet paper with

no slots for the roll.
Sorry made of birdsong.
Thank the Carolina wren

who pecks our smallest seeds.
Thank the jay
who won't wait in line

for ancient grains.
Sorry made of blossoms
and better days.

Raw

"Unix has its own flavors,"
says Lou. I shouldn't

find this sexy. Then
he starts in on

"raw coding," and I'm
hooked.

We're viewing math
porn, a superset of Python

fireworks across the
screen. Lou claims,

"See, you can change
gravity!" Sheep

and red wolves
surge through blue air.

Then something about
turtle logos,

unverified.
"Signals are

everywhere," Lou says.
Tell me about it.

"But this assumes two
agents are rational."

My pet, I
assure you,

they are not.

Your Call

If you want a love poem, you'll have to
write it, Sweetie.

He's sitting on his married ass.
Not that I've really

looked—my eyesight's not
what it was.

Still, even half-blind I can spot
sinewy,

agile and damn it,
a poet! Translate

him into another tongue.
Soften the blow. (Note to self: don't say "blow"

in lines about him.) Stick with
flat words, no tongue.

If Neruda were here, in my mouth,
he'd say, *Quiero.*

Don't say mouth.
Cite elbows, neutral parts.

No long *O*'s.
We all want, baby.

He's all email and no flesh.
If he fires off one poem a month,

you're luckier than most.
O taste & swallow!

No calories, no
regrets.

Not Even

I want what I do not have,
Pablo.
Is that a First World problem?

Not (even) enough
love
for a scar, he laughed.

My love kept inviting me in.
Then he erased
the door.

You're no kid,
Pablo said.
And he has four.

Don't (even) write
about crossing
the line,

(Unless)
you're ready
to pay

the ferry
todos. The
mortal price.

Nothing Good Can Come

Your wife was right.
You were dreaming
me. You promised her
no more porn and no more
teacher fan-boy.

Sky omens agreed:
ironic blue, no touch of you-
and-me.
The clouds moved on.
I should, too.

If

If I loved him more, they'd have to lock me up,
I sang, and the air sneered,

Nah, not even worth a
cuff.

Give him time, time,
I said. He's agile, strong.

And he has a thing
for teachers.

You're retired, the air
yawned.

But mental things alone are real,
I complained. A real poet wrote that.

Blake was wrong,
air scoffed, real

nut job.

All We Did Not Share

> *we will always draw life*
> *from all we did not share*
> (Neruda)

I'm midway
through an epic about not tasting word
from you, *nada*.

Once, inside flowery May,
we wove couplets.

I got hooked. At lines' end, I
craved more.

Dark fire,
the lack of letters

stings most, invisible briars. I'm
watering them.

Dante, help! When there was no
Beatrice, when you met

lit absence—
how did you breathe?

Honestly, Buddy,
one glimpse and you fed

for the rest of your
exiled life? I inch

like a millipede, aching
for a syllable

before
being squashed.

Signore, were you never sore at Bea
for lacking flesh?

Never pissed
she didn't write back?

Hell's my cell phone
with no message from you.

Too trendy?
Tantalus break–

dances my skull
in mourning

air. Silence slices
like the good knife.

What love survives that?
Pablo, you would have forged

an ode
to the blade.

More

Make it more sensual so I can grasp it.
Okay, say we were born

in the same century.
We kissed so hard our mouths

might break. We tried slow,
but we were more like a B flick

where two dive
and moan.

Rise and rose.
Tall tree.

We listened with our bodies.
Word made flesh.

Get it? Buddy,
you would.

Small Song

There's quiet when he
stops speaking
to me

and in the blanks
I begin again.
Listen.

The air hums
and the bravest birds
swoop through the frosted bushes

as if tying
a ribbon
on today.

Let go of sorrow,
indifference,
cruelty.

Find someone else
with his name
and give away

the signed books.
Make of love
an unburdening,

a potlatch, a brag:
My losses are
spectacular,

bold,
like a
woman

walking away.

II. Letters From Earth and Sky

Breakfast in Paris

They're playing "Sounds of Silence"
at *le petit dejeuner,* and man,

I know that tune,
those soundless notes

I hear from you.
No royalties on these blues.

How do you say "Come back!"
in your *langue*?

They're spinning our
ballad, buddy,

and even a mouthful
of this Parisian croissant

can't calm my tongue.
O taste & swallow the bitter coffee.

I'll wrap your silence
in my silk scarf, my *foulard,*

crooning the sounds
of a woman alone in Paris.

Not Edith Piaf,
not Barbara,

just me, Tennessee,
wailing those mean

hound dog
blues.

Rain

It rains in my heart—see
Verlaine. Not a medical condition.

Tread-mark on the back road.
You want rhyme, Monsieur?

It's a toad. Other denizens find
this charming. It rains in my heart,

la la la. Yesterday was junior high,
all day, through the night.

Go buy an umbrella and walk off
that fat ass,

bloated sentiments.
The blues cannot be bought off.

In Paris, they will escort you
arm-in-arm to the Seine.

Take another fat slice of *mon
coeur, monsieur.*

It doesn't rain in my heart,
but it's humid.

Fifty Shades of Gluten

He said he would beat me with a baguette when I got home, and
I wanted to say, yes, please.

So much depends upon good manners.
Don't bite the baguette that beats you.

Madame corrects me—her cat is a boy.
"Used to be!" Claude snorts.

Still thinking about that long
loaf.

Famished.
And he is young and married.

And so am I (married

So (not-young

What Now

What are you planning to write,
now that he's dead? Silence asked.

He's not dead, he's
just quiet, I said.

Silence pushed back, covering
my toes like tide coming in,

ankles, thighs.
I'm faithful sexy, Silence said.

Who's crying? My cheek
stings, wet.

Silence keeps laughing
in my face.

You're not crazy,
Rimbaud said.

He chose commerce
over song

in the end.
Hey, write one alexandrine

as fine as mine, Arty said,
then you can throw those

cute little stones.

Best Case

"Oh, I could drink a case of you—"
you as 2005

Bordeaux,
no ordinary red.

I'd savor you on the sly,
take my time.

You wouldn't last long.
Now I'm sipping air

like a fucked-up fish.
I want you here.

I want to do to you
what the Garonne does

to lovers who swim naked
despite Sunday laws,

take you down-
stream,

buoy you all the way to Spain.
I don't want to swallow a river,

just you,
your undammable

overflow.

Garonne Love

I've come back to
     you dear
fatal river
     stirring
dreams &
     memories *je*
reviens and
     today you
don't pretend
     to be calm.
Your surface trembles
     shifting
skin—
     how I love you
here
     & here.

I like for you
     to be absent, sure,
but present
     would be
sweet, too.
     I could
show you a thing
     or two, sir,
about trembling,
     & flow.

Feather

Sure, it's only a pigeon feather,
not a message from him.
The iridescent sheen will remind me

of these cobblestone streets,
uneven pathways,
dangerous, picturesque.

All I wanted was a line.
Sky left me a feather,
white point, quill,

back in the day.
Back when he wrote to me,
when blank space wasn't where

words should be.
Did Beatrice ever dream Dante?
Who am I in this tale?

Love-crazed poet,
light-headed femme?
Pigeon,

lonesome dove?
Weightless time,
Attendez!

The breeze
transports his
handsome voice

to a younger,
firmer
shore.

Couvre-feu

Means "curfew."
Literally, cap

the fire.
Cool it. Stay

back. For
years,

I had to cover
what I felt.

Tasteless
now, to

compare
love with deadly

germs. So
I'll put a lid

on it.
"Stay safe,"

we say, as if
anyone

would choose
to uncap

flame, to
stay deadly.

"Choose life,"
the Jewish saying goes.

I chose
Lou. So,

this poem
turns out to be

about
wedlock—

about my hub, who
rants loudly

at the other
desktop.

That's life these
days.

All the secrets
have been

crushed,
sealed,

swallowed.

Dear Lichen,

Thank you for today's letter on bark, reminding me
that humans and plants interconnect.

"Dear Marilyn, I am not lichen, I am moss. Be more
precise in your loving. Remember those

mistakes you made
in the Sixties?"

Dear Moss, Alas, yes,
some errors were not merely grammatical.

Take the two Pierres
at the Cité Universitaire.

One called me his *fiancée*.
Another led me to the *corrida* in Seville

when the bull ring was empty. Even our mistakes stir
reveries. *"Ça commence à se mettre*

en place, Mademoiselle," pronounced the kindly
Professeur de Civilisation. "It's a start."

Hélas, there was also mean Monsieur Foutre,
who spat, "You have learned nothing, Mademoiselle!"

I said *"la"* instead of *"les,"*
complained about his mother-in-law's penny-pinching.

I was her student boarder. She pressed her ear
to the bathroom door, to assess who used

too much water. Served thin soup,
and once, *hérisson*.

"Wrong, Monsieur!" I responded.
I have learned never to eat hedgehog,

no matter how cheap, how slow
in the forest. And to be kind to strangers,

kinder than you,
Monsieur Motherfucker!

Let the Phantoms Go

Our lives are packed with phantoms, noisy ones,
clowns, braggards, bastards
and friendly guys. Or else
our lives are riddled with pheasants.

Can't quite grasp the sense of this
article in *Le Monde.*
Whatever, they are ferocious and persistent.
Hard to feed them in this economy.

We writers host tragic phantoms,
or pheasants, who eat us out of house,
or they are mediocre electricians,
elevated by history.

The stern bakery lady refused to put the *tartelette*
in a box. Why? Because I said *"le"* and not *"la"*?
"Ah, non!" she groaned.
She was rushed perhaps by phantoms,

busy ones, envious, premeditated,
or by pheasants who eat her grain at night.
Soaked in *"syrope d'Arabel"* whatever that is.
"It's like caramel," the lady at the next table said,

spun by airy *belles,*
seductive and powerful as ravens, errant souls.

First World Problems

Why are lost things always the most beautiful? The black silk scarf with gold trim that I bought in New Orleans and sported daily— where is it now? I spilled Lagavulin on it and remember thinking that was possibly an omen, tried to correct my melancholy, superstitious mind. No, the plane would not fall out of the sky. Though my travel cell came with a user's manual in ancient Babel.

I remember whining that the scarf had turned into a ribbon. Now I want it back, that tie at my neck that tethered me gently to appearances and the moment. I used to leave the house as if I was wrapped for the world.

When I scored the goods on Chartres, I had not yet given a poetry reading next to pinball machines at The Gold Mine. The scarf was my token of hope. Pretty and unique, I had found it for a price, the way a hunter goes loaded for prey and comes home with meat or fur.

Was I beautiful when I wore it? Who am I with nothing at my neck but time?

I remember taking it off at the McAllister's after three or four Pousse-Rapières. When I asked if I had left it there, Niles said yes, but he handed me an umbrella. I laughed and said I was lucky that I had only left that much. I felt like a wronged monkey, indignant at the poor substitute.

Now I'm obsessed with what I left behind. I'm rolling around in loss like a puppy in mud. I have become the one lost. I gambled my scrap of mortality and lost.

Are You Sure?

You want to delete this?
These images
will go blotto.

Sure?
Yes, delete.
I fall apart.

Nowhere is the image
of me with Shakespeare's cat
in my lap.

No Marilyn Hacker humming
into the bookstore mike.
I was introduced

as "a very famous poet."
Then my host said, "but I can't
remember her credits."

What magic makes the deleted
disappear? I didn't
delete my father,

but I never see him.
He died before deleting
was an option.

Calm down, Mar,
It was only an album!
I looked ecstatic

with purring Agatha
at Shakespeare and Co.
Chantal all smiles as if we were friends.

Reform Jews don't pray for photos
to be undeleted.
We pray for the strength

to make more memories
and books,
better friends.

Adam

If I loved you more, they'd have to
lock me up. I should thank you

for distracting me from
the ticking under my tee,

bless you for the bait-and-switch,
urgent notes, surge

of poems you pumped out,
right before you

braked. If you could distract me
from you, we'd have a

win-win. As it stands,
I've been kicked out of

Paradise again.
It was a painted backdrop,

but man!
You were the prototype,

it seemed.

Ode to a Dogwood Bud

I tried to snap you,
Little Beauty,

to bring you in.
You wouldn't bend.

I adore shape
that doesn't

shatter or fold.
Keats's urn stays

"still unravish'd"
in the mind.

But that fishy dude
I told you about, the poet?

Catfishing, more sullen
than *Henri le chat*—

"*Pourquoi?* Why do they
brush me?"

Talk about frenzy, "mad
pursuit!"

Had to brush him off,
nip the buds, break

the nuts
to save the tree.

Experimental

You want
a bulletproof vest

with breathing room.
No poem

residue.
Instead of Grandma, press

one Cossack horseshoe
in dust.

Insert Yiddish phrase
only God

knows.
Erase.

Make it
gleam.

Add lip
gloss, no

pork.

Practicing

You think because he's practicing goodbye he won't leave. Maybe
it's a story and the ending is made of words. When you press, he
mentions working on revisions. If he splits, you'll repaint the
empty halls and doorframes. You'll put his nuts and bolts in
storage. Call Good Will. Call the Industrial Blind. Rope your car
around the dead bush he's attached to and yank it out. You'll feel
emptier than Hades after Orpheus and Eurydice moved out. "Go
with him!" Vivian says. "He's a good-looking man and some
woman will latch onto him." His life is revision. Yours may get
whited out. Get a jump on the empyrean, grab a taste of the void.
Vive Verlaine! Start drinking absinthe. Start now.

Dismissed

"I'm not looking at you!"
the hawk shrieks.
"Where's that cute
red–headed
chipmunk?"

Days when even
Nature mocks,
don't summon
Seventh Grade snubs.
Think about Mister
Murphy, your English
teacher, who advised you not
to hang with Sal Noto,
that you deserved
respect.

Don't think about Mickey,
who threatened to
stab himself with a steak
knife, because you
wouldn't pet.
Summon
Baudelaire, who
distilled darkness,
decanted tears
for the page
like fine wine.
Stay drunk on words.

Don't think about hash.
You tried the pipe,

once, 1968,
dreamed your dorm
was ablaze.
Think about the
delicate Sancerre
you stashed in the closet
upstairs. Later, maybe,
after the two online
poetry readings.

The hawk grows bored.
His golden chest is warm.
He's focused on his
prey, the way
you should hunt for
sounds.
When the low
heavy sky
breaks your heart,
don't think about
the cliquish hallway at
Oceanside Junior
High. Thank
Mister Murphy
for saving Seventh Grade
with books
and poems.
He was a boxer,
like Donne
with consonants.
"Batter my heart"
shouldn't make you
think of chocolate babka.

Don't dream about
a younger man,
unless you
mean your hard-
working
hub.

Reader, every day
I marry
only
him.
One
long-burning
fire, one.

Letters from Earth & Sky

Petals
on the earth
and William Stafford
say it best:
You are not alone.
The dogwoods
stand, jays screech
improv
with the hawks.
Yesterday,
the neighbors'
black Lab
came racing by
for a caress,
and you could hear
your own
shameless
heart.

So wrap yourself in
hope & a mask
and walk—greet
that family at
the end
of the block.

Silky
petals
drop
like divine notes,
& no one
gets

hurt—be
like that,
soft,
kind.

Read that tiny
ant-memo, crawling
on your glasses
while you write:
You are not alone.

Rimbaud
was wrong: I
is not "someone else."
I is all of us,
on a stroll to meet
the new, the guileless,
and the oldest
blossoming trees—

long-flowering ones
we yearn to sing
& become.

III. Sing the Unsung

Ode to Ragweed

Knoxville, Tennessee

Ragweed, you have turned my sinuses into I-40 Westbound
    on a Friday afternoon.
You morphed my song into early Bob Dylan.
You changed my cash into crumpled tissues and Benadryl.
You bankrolled my doctor's kids through Duke, through
    Vanderbilt.
You wave your green handkerchief and I
    bow and cough my forced tribute.
You have raised Knoxville to Number Three on the allergy hit
    parade!
Ragweed, you are queen of a humid kingdom and you
    have created a hamlet of snot—to breathe
    or not to breathe?
Poets need air, Ragweed! We beseech you:
    carry your pollen out to sea!
Let salt be your Muhammad Ali,
    the blow that sends you
    down for the count,
    Ragweed!

The Morels

They were a neighborhood
family of mushrooms

living right down by
the side of the house.

I would have trampled
them, but my ecologist

spouse tenderly
brought them in,

cleaned, then
fried them in butter

and Sauvignon Fumé.
A heady smell arose,

woodsy flavors
emerged from the pan.

Those knobby ones
urged me to taste

more. Sure, we're
cloistered, closed in,

but the morels
made me see that Freud

wasn't wrong. I mean,
look at them, poking up

out of the ground
like that.

The Biggest Blue Jay

Lives in the hedge next door.
I have hedge envy.

He swoops in once daily
when I set out

crumbs. Four times per,
if I drop seeds or multi-grain

bits. Passover begins
tomorrow, so we'll see

if whole-wheat matzo warrants
his indigo flight.

I am in love with a bird,
whom Lou does not envy.

He's a secure guy.
When I confessed that I write to

a poet once a week, the
Air Force dude, Lou

didn't blink. 39 years,
and he's serene about love.

The only thing we argue
in our suburban fort

is how to fold the
hand towels.

Also, whether to watch
"All Rise" or

"A French Village."
I gave him that rerun.

I'll name the jay
Beau: *"O les beaux jours*

de bonheur
indicible…"

"Oh the fine days
of unspeakable joy."

Hélas, Verlaine, these
unspeakable days

are not carefree.
Tell Rimbaud we're done.

I am thankful to be cooped
with a good man,

grateful that the blues
have wings.

Correspondences

In the driveway, fallen bark
drafts notes to the cherry leaves,
the way I compose daily songs
for you, with my life, my
body. The bark &
leaves speak quietly, in the
language of colors—aqua and
lacy lichen, dressed
for a wedding. My
driveway reads
like a Romantic poem—
says beauty persists, that
we owe trees and sky an
apology, that love can be
quiet or shout out, that we must
work to heal the fallen
while there's time.

Sometimes, Thinking About Art

(Arthur Smith, 1948–2018)

"Sometimes nothing helps," you wrote.
None of us believed that.
We thought love, good dogs,
modern medicine, cuttings
that stayed crisp.
We thought poetry and we
were right about that.

I think no, you can't be
gone. Some cuttings
are too cruel.
The terror
you felt was
swept by love, swifts,
great loss—
ours, now.

Anyone Can

"Anyone can write
six lines," Art Smith
said. So he did,
each dawn. "They don't have
to be good. Just get out
of your own way."

Keats crooned, "Seasons
of mist" & who knows what
when the muse wasn't
on tap. Shelley
might have toasted
crows on an off-day.

And Shakespeare?
"That time of year…"
is here, now, big
time, like a mallet
over us, playing
whack-a-mole with lungs

and germs. Corona
sounds good, sounds
beautiful, a crown.
But crowns
are not always
a good sign. The one

with thorns—no
royal holiday.
Those I'll

need on my teeth,
pricey. Shakespeare
never wailed

about sore molars.
Who would listen?
That rotten year,
in my gums,
in my country's polity.
The oaks drop

gold notes on the lawn.
They don't have to
be pulled.
Six lines.
The page knows
its own gravity.

Sing the Unsung

My horoscope commands,
"Sing the unsung
today."

Wonder what Homer's
stars spelled
the day he launched

The Odyssey. "Sing
the wine. No, scratch
that! Sing

the wine-dark
sea. Leave
arms and the man and

Helen to Virgil."
"Fukk that!" Homer
growled, wove

Penelope into the
long song
spelled out

by Orion
and Venus,
after a stellar meet

that also spawned
Rimbaud,
Lucille Clifton,

Adrienne, Bill Stafford,
Joy Harjo, & all
the daring young, plus

silvery bards &
ageless ones, home
now, worker bees

humming,
sweetening
time

with music,
rescoring the
sad universe,

syllable by
stirring
sounds.

Spiderwort

I'll call you violet-heart,
petit-pansy-
contender,
purple earth-alum,
plum welcome,
silky hand,
one who was picked,
flutters joy,
never
asks
for donations.

Who names a sprout
spiderwort?
Ultra-violet, your
budding light
brightens
my cloistered days.
Delicate letter
from the earth,
I read you, soft
& clear. Should have
had a crush
on you
instead of that
built dude.

To the Wizard in Fallen Bark

Dogwood, bark, I hear
your *entendre*.
Clever! Love what
you've done
with the lichen
collar. *Très elegant!*
And the two eyes
set on one side—
double the odds for
a seer!

Soon, I'll
put you back on
the lawn with your
buds. Take a message
to the earth: tell
her that blooms
have saved us
this spring. We
frail peeps are stuck
in place. But you
show beauty
shaped
in place, offer
hand-outs
on
being
rooted.

Cucumber Magnolia Leaf

Whoever named you never met a cucumber.
You're more bronze-medal leaf,
grander than others on the ground.
You glow like midsummer night,
your skin flecked with tan,
like a Valley girl.
You survived rain and cold—
you're a shield,
warrior leaf.

Lighter.
Your glow is magical,
possible. Gerard Manley
Hopkins signed
you with his breath.
You're a shapely raft
for elves and ladybugs.
Your sheen holds the gold
of backyard days in childhood,
when Lady was still alive,
biting the neighbor boys,
but never Mommy. Her fingers
smelled of Alpo.
Her red nails were perfect,
a Saturday habit
that can't have been
cheap. She was competing
with Marjorie Molliver,
the saleslady at dad's party store,
"Fun at Home,"
who smacked of
Liz Taylor.

Earthly glow, you never need
to compete. You were painted
by autumn, by beyond-our-
control. Your cracked
face cannot help but remind
us of a mask. No fault.
Those breaks let us glimpse
half-light,
the magic world. When
I read this poem through
the cracks, the flaws,
I see, "mother,
perfect, a habit."

I'm in love with a leaf.
Easier than
talking with some.
Your golden sheen does not
make you snobby or gruff.
Your curves call up "Mother
Earth." The smallest hole
in your crisp skin lets us
view myriad stars, those
hiding until
dark, and we see.

Mean time,
we peek through this golden-
bronze fan, made for
elves and sprites—
not for cucumbers or
fat legumes of any
sort.

Treasure

I search for one gold leaf—
not the kind men
crave, but a silken
teardrop, loose
leaf wish—yours,
young black cherry,
prunus serotina.
You know nothing of
human misery.

Yours is not
the willful
"epistemology of ignorance,"
not a history of
bad choices and one
red-face
raging stump.
You don't crave
words—just
sun, rain,
wind in your
leaves, &
you have all you
need. I read you,
soft & clear.

Word turns
"treasure"
to "tears."
Little serrated leaf, you
harm no one,
enrich no coffers.

You're a slip of hope,
gold gleam
amid grass.
Autocorrect opts for
"god"
instead of
"gold." Not bad, Word,
not Perfect, but
not bad.

Ode to Our Backyard Possum

I named him
Marvin, to turn

the tale of a dude
I dated, eons

ago, a *schlub.*
Shlemozzel.

Upstate. Not prison,
hot-shot Liberal Arts.

He was fat, articulate,
wouldn't wear a sleeve.

Before the pill.
His hair was Bryl-Cream

slick,
schnoz flat.

Bragged the highest IQ
on campus. But

wouldn't wear an
inconvenient skin.

Putz!
In the end, I was

mean.
I won't be rude

to Marvin the
Possum, who is

harmless,
sweet. Marvena?

She scavenges
toast. The blue jays

feast on
multi-grains with seeds,

like health-food
groupies.

We can turn
the narrative.

If not,
there's voodoo.

Make a Marv doll
from marshmallows,

toast until golden.
Dip in melted

chocolate
and feed the prize to

your good hub.
Lick his lips.

Hand him
a napkin,

if this
is a family poem.

Next

"the next sentient being
on deck, me,"

or Buffy, who watched us
pull away from Lebron
Avenue.
Later, Mommy told
me our dog died
of mange,
"neglect."

Buffy, the first
sentient being I
loved.
"We had no choice,"
Mommy said,
"the buyers wanted her
with the house."

Alternate:
"We're going to New York,
an apartment might not
take us with a dog."
Or with
a little girl?

We pulled away—
that's me, sad, sad,
warm-blooded
without words,
the next sentient being

trashed
on the
lawn.

Returns

You know my story, how
we got kicked out of Montgomery—
in my father's version, it
was always "a miscarriage of
justice," as if justice was a bloody
baby. The big corps came after Daddy.
His watches were outselling Swiss brands,
American Merchandising must close down.
We had to scram, or the D.A. would toss
Grandma Stella in jail.

Or maybe a clerk stalled the returned
merch, for spite.
As time ran on, we
had to run.

Returns.
We go back
and back.
Show me again
why we were spit out
from what Mommy called heaven.
Our spaniel ditched
on the lawn.
Buffy!
Her sad eyes
follow me. No,
This time
I won't abandon

her
golden,
breathing
body.

Starter Bra

Grandma Stella
fitted me,

soft cotton,
34B.

I didn't make it past
the starting gate.

Boys didn't mind.
Buds

were enough.
Tender tips.

"Enough!"
my mother cried,

shipped me to Paris
to pry me

from the hippy
starter-boyfriend.

It worked,
and didn't.

He flew over to see me.
Then something

fell
out of the air

between us.
The next semester,

he escorted another girl
to French Poetry.

Okay, Mommy was right.
She was busty, my

Ma. Dad, Army Private
First Class, could not stay

private when she offered
him a cold Coca-Cola.

in her Montgomery
drawl. He was a Brooklyn boy.

You know most
of the rest.

How the round ones
near my heart

swelled when
my baby was born.

Heather made me promise
never to read aloud

that poem about
her nursing on me.

Poets slam
promises

night &
day.

Ode to the Silvery Pillowcase

I snagged you at the Dollar Store,
but you gather the room

like a cotton duenna,
a two-buck Martha Stewart

non-felony touch. You ask
nothing of me, lend sheen

to this lonely artist-colony habitat.
You remind me that I have taste,

a yearning for beauty, here,
in Falwell country.

That even if no one speaks to me at dinner,
I can lay my head down in pride

and peace. Silver flag of domesticity,
you were made

on the cheap, but you soothe me.
Your elegance recalls my

mother, how she shopped thrift
when we were poor, scored our threadbare

Persian rug and had me ink in
the bald spots when I was eight.

I'm still filling in blanks,
aiming to revive what's faded.

You gleam like treasure,
like a loving-cup,

like *Shabbos* candles,
and my mother's hands,

lighting them.
Good night, silvery pillowcase.

Come back, dreams!
Silvery ink,

rewrite us
into a gentler world.

IV. If Love Whispers

Removed

March 19, 2012

At the Franciscan friary all the news is apple blossoms,
the white opossum, ghosts in the historic barn.

I'm too removed, won't be reminded
of anti-Semitism, fresh murders in Belle France.

The gunman blasted a paratrooper,
three French soldiers, then a teacher and three children

at Ozar Hatorah, their Jewish elementary school.
Toulouse lies an hour from our workshop in Auvillar,

further from this friary in rural Indiana.
Bullets don't ricochet

overseas. The anti-Semitism that killed keeps killing. I'm
removed. Here the news is Eastern Bluebirds.

I don't hear shooting, jihadists.
Won't write about Paris gendarmes, cheered

by the Gestapo. The *rafles*—roundups,
not winning tickets. July, 1942,

Drancy. 2012, the French come to terms:
cardboard memorials,

a lone railway car.
The plaza hosts a circus and drug deals.

Drancy. Septfonds.
Auschwitz.

What I do know.

No One

No one talked about *les juifs,*
French anti-Semitism
when I was in school.
No mention of Vel d'Hiv,
more than 13,000 rounded up,
4000 children. No one said, Drancy,
Septfois, Auschwitz.
Gung-ho gendarmes.

In September, 1941,
Parisians were on high alert
for sneaky Jews.
"Comment reconnaitre le Juif?."
Get your anti-Semitic cue cards
at the Palais Berlitz!
Half-a-million visitors can't
be wrong.
How to recognize a Jew?
The talons, the spidery greed!
In case you missed it, here's "Jewry
Feasting on the Blood of
Our France."

The first I heard of this
was at the dinner table in Paris,
Avenue du Parc Montsouris, 1966,
when Monsieur M. laughed about the day
the Paris police arrived at his factory
"and took away the Jews."
I was nineteen, a student boarder,
kept my mouth shut, except to eat.

Palais Berlitz was only a palace if you
loved Vichy France. Anti-Semitism
is over, right? The Pope says
no. The graffiti on Eli Weisel's birthplace
splashes no. Steve Bannon's crew
laughs aloud. Jews
were "the enemy of the people" then.

I didn't taste anti-Semitism with my
croissant until I supped at Monsieur's table.
You don't have to be the Pope
to choke on today's hate-laced air.

Violins of Hope, Knoxville

1.
I don't blame you for hope,
For wanting violins.

For the Schwarzes of Horb,
There were no elegant sounds,

No quivering long notes.
Deportation came

Crashing & swift.
But for Hedwig, there was air.

The nameless angel who rescued
Her broken body from the

Transport car hurried her to
Marienhospital, where

The Sisters treated the only Jew
With silence.

The Just man who lifted her
From the rails

Offered hope, the key
To staying human.

Each violin reminds us
That silence is no remedy

For persecution.

2.

My maiden name was Zimmerman.
This first violin is my kin.

Thin and hungry, it calls
From another country.

Its wood remembers the forest,
Does not tremble

The way humans shook
In '38, in '41.

Each violin is a cradle
For one voice, for millions.

Each seasoned instrument
Resounds with

History—shtetls and ghettos,
Liberation.

This violin was a lifeline
For awhile, a coin

To feed the family.
For another, a ticket out.

Torn, one violin
Awakens others,

Replanted here,
A forest of sounds.

3.
Of all instruments, the violin
Comes closest to the human voice.

I hear the Schwarzes of Horb
Praying, right before

Rifles fired through the Black Forest,
Through Bikernieki.

These violins were witnesses
All over Europe,

Where string sections were growing thin,
And the musicians, thinner.

Each violinist is a witness,
Sorrow pouring through a lyrical body.

Gripped by these sounds,
We too bear witness

To hope thrust from a train window,
Stirring in the pit

Of the orchestra,
Rising above strife.

This harmony is not easy.
We must continue to speak out

Against graffiti, strains of hate.
This violin was filled with ashes.

This violin was restored
And handed to a young musician

Who practiced hope daily,
Who learned to wake the world again.

Coda:
Perlman
Mintz
Heifetz
Menuhin
Stern
Zuckerman

Names
The poem breathes—
In them,
Heaven.

Love Song to the Kind Ones

This is a love song to the
Sister of Mercy who sat with me
for hours in the waiting room,

while my sister was being born.
She flipped *Life Magazine* to a full
spread of Nabisco cookies,

and we waited together, while I
drooled. Where was Dad?
I was three. No one questioned me

about my faith.
Cookies and Sister
calmed me. This is a love song

to that patient, robed one,
& to my baby sis.
Not so little now, she

keeps me company
in poetry, in our epic
calls. I ship Georgia peaches

north, for her June birthday.
This is a love song to kindness,
to moments when sweet ones

lend a hand. A love song
to the next generation, the
tiniest ones,

jelly beans with heartbeats.
This is my hopeful call to
to the

new, let's-be-more-human
beings.

No Egg, No Pony

Easter Sunday afternoon, Nassau County hosted an egg hunt.
The winning child would score a pony. A real pony! We were
mud poor, could barely feed ourselves and Cindy, our shaggy
mutt. Jewish kids didn't hunt for eggs, we ate them. Passover, we
searched for the *afikomen*. But that day we were all in. Mommy
drove me to the amphitheater where the hunt for a pony began.
I was six. I found dust and fancy-dressed kids. No egg. Maybe it
was jammed in a politician's pocket? Someone must have won.
I wailed. What would we have done with a pony? We could only
afford rent for part of our house. Rudy, the owner, The Drunk,
lived in the upstairs guest room until we finally ditched him and
the Montgomery Grandma moved in. That night, Daddy brought
home a magic slate from the Brooklyn candy store. I drew
Mommy, Daddy, my baby sister and three little pigs looking for
payback. I pressed too hard on the slate, scratched my name in
block letters. Etched a ghost-pony who didn't need pockets
or food.

The New York Grandma Disputes Marcus Aurelius

"Nothing lasts forever
or even for
very long,"
Marcus Aurelius opined.

"*Oy*, he didn't know
your Uncle Harry!"
Grandma said.
"His stories were

snoozers, and
he passed gas
at the table.
Marcus are-you-nuts

didn't know Cossacks,
how long
we hid.
No joke.

Marcus the Billious
never got
packed into
steerage

for Ellis
Island."
"But you got here,
Grandma!

Look at the bright
side!" "*Oy!*" Grandma
said, it was dark
for a very

long time.
Aurelius was
a *schlemelius.* Ask
your Uncle Nat

how long
steel bars lasted
in Sing Sing.
Ask the East River

how long
it took to sink
his guns,
ask the ones

riddled
down."
"Stop it, Grandma,
we need hope!"

"*Oy,* hope!
The cockroaches
on Coney Island
had hope.

Ask my guitar
stashed on top of
the hall closet
how long it waited.

Sometimes I play
when no one
hears. In secret, I strum
Yiddish songs

and my heart
rejoins the beat.
Secrets run long.
Music echoes

over steppes,
past pogroms.
And love?
I am still holding

my baby daughter,
my sons. And
the mothballs
from my

second-hand
store are
staving off
hungry

enemies,
keeping
your little wool coat
safe,

in case by some miracle
there's a great-grandbaby,
and a better moving
day."

Dear Marilyn

"I enjoyed your poem, 'Jim Out of Prison,'
but I do not believe in the 'you'
of your song.
I'm in for a dime at Rahway.
Comparing your life as a woman
with that of a prisoner
is absurd,
with all due respect."
(Rahway State Prison, 1974)

Dear Prisoner, you nailed it.
There was no "you,"
just a series of bad decisions.
Some of them were good poets,
some had good hair.
Love? Can't find it
in the lines.

Back then I stayed
blue, but no one
shackled me. Marty liked to be tied up,
not the point.
Sure, there was a forced
marriage, but the food was good
on East 18th,
and there was no guard—unless
you count my mother.

I apologize to any prisoners I have offended
with off-handed metaphors
depicting marriage as lockup,

knives-in-the-shower, apologize
for the word "rape,"
which should never be used as metaphor.

So here we are.
This husband is real, a full-on "you."
If Dante seems less real, fault
my poetry, which
adores him as if
he could love me back.
"As if" buys us dead air.

I hope you're free now, my
sharp prisoner,
my critic. You were right about everything.
By now you have your name back.
Write to me.
I won't compete, or pretend
to understand.

Dictation From the Hawk

"I found today's object!"
Lou cheered, waved

a hawk's feather, the kind
an English gentleman

might have dipped in ink,
back when.

White and brown,
the stripes wave

like painted water,
earth & sky, rippling.

Two smiles and an eye
etch the quill.

The eye-slit seems wary,
that of a snake

or fairytale villain.
At the kitchen table, when I hone

in, my mother blinks
the oven light. Jealous

of a feather? "Keep it light!"
the feather warns.

"Remember that high-priced
Jungian in San Diego?

June Singer! She fell asleep
during your session. When you

called her out, she sighed,
'You were talking about your mother

again.'" Not even 300 bucks
could keep her awake.

The red-shouldered hawk
had a mother, too—

so agile she birthed plumes
that swooped

& soared. Keep it light,
or the hawk

might charge you
by the hour.

Write love songs and silly
lines about Herbie the roach

and Marvin the possum,
not the ballad of your Mama blinking

green eyes at your Private
First Class dad, not his rage and fear.

Not bankruptcy. Not
the Joey Gallo

story. Just two smiles,
whispery. Write

a feather, tickling.
Help the poem forget.

A couplet should not
require an attorney.

Not every poem calls
for last will,

breath,
testament.

Ode to Herbie, the Big One

Herbie was not my first cockroach,
but he was big, fat as a mouse.

He lounged in a corner of the
downstairs bath

and we communed.
Lost track.

You know how that
goes—the guy you

had a crush on from
school stops

writing back. Then, lo!
Dude wants a letter of

recommendation or
an alibi. Anyway, today

Herbie scooted out
from under the toaster oven.

He had been thriving
on multigrain bagel bits,

gleamed, glossy,
successful, like a

Seventies College
Avenue pimp.

My hub
coaxed him onto

a copy of *West
Knoxville Lifestyle,*

relocated the Grandee
to our lawn. We tossed

farewell crumbs.
Now he'll have to race

the jays.
As for the ex-crush,

we wish him well
in his new life.

"All lives, all dances,
and all is loud!" the Gabon sing.

Maybe.
All but that guy.

May he find
his voice, apologize.

Mean time,
we listen

for jays
and cricket wings,

recall Herbie's
farewell drops,

sprinkled
like text

in the
feed.

The Moth Widow's Song

When I split for the ceiling he seemed fine,
flapping around Special K in the
stove where we nested, in
peanuts, among shells.
We were peaceful,
private residents,
nibbled rotting raisins.

On the day I opted for the
wider world, lured by the bright
kitchen light, my moth boy
opted to stay home in cardboard.
He was never one to run around.
Then, with no warning, some
hairy-handed yeti

flipped on the oven.
Skip the historical analogies,
not my forte.
I am the moth's wife, a pro
at transformation, normally
an optimist.
My whirr's so quiet

you won't hear me
before you spy my silk.
Now I cling to the papered wall,
to the memory
of another so delicate, so fine,
he fanned me
into ecstasy.

Glint

Moonlight
hit my teaspoon,
but the editor wanted more,

demanded the throaty
chirp of wrens
and the migration route

of geese and Balthic
Orioles. Sought
bullies down,

dead masters and ghost slaves,
mounds and unmarked
graves in backwoods

Amherst County. My
humble teaspoon
cried, Give me a break!

And then
it fed me
song.

If Love Whispers

You can't say, "Every day is a wound,"
while bones are being
shattered.

Silence is huge, but don't
strap Moby Dick
to your ballad.

Don't beg.
Respect
those

in need.
You can wait
in yourself

like a shadow.
If love whispers,
listen. If

love shouts, send
it to its room.
Your body

is love's room.
Listen.
Take dictation.

If love cries, "I
want out!" find
someone

unafraid. Become
the blaze
you craved.

Now that You Ask, Emily,

I'm Nobody Two.
I can't rhyme like you,
have no hymn to lean on,
just bare bones.

So? Now that I'm Nobody
I can howl like Petey
The Beagle at the moon.
We heard him wail

down Vincent Street.
Did he long
for a caress? A bone?
He couldn't connect

on the internet.
Neither could you,
Miss D. You wrapped
yourself in pure poetry.

In your cameo,
I spy lace. Word
just changed "spy" to "spay."
Never fear, Petey!

You're free from harm now.
Some eves, the moon
still rises full
on night's thighs.

Harvest Moon, they called it,
at Camp Cayuga Happy Land.
With moonlit memories,
I will never be alone, saved

from thirteen-year-old angst
by that undimmable light that
led us to the Harvest Moon
Ball in the gym.

Girls could go solo,
or with friends. I strolled over
with my bud, Caren.
Counselors-in-Training,

we asked the boys to dance,
Ladies Choice,
all night long.
Handsome Dave got sent home

for peeing in his bed.
Or for making out with Jodie.
Joel from Bronx High
School of Science wasn't much

of a catch. We hopped the Lindy
together, Car and I,
forgot our blues,
her parents' divorce,

Joey Gallo's
threats against my dad.
We rocked, and she named
her next puppy Cha Cha.

I can't be Nobody yet,
wrapped in memories.
Lit skies and slow dances
hang like paper lanterns.

Petey, we'll dedicate
our next moonlight stroll
to you. You were more
faithful than boys we knew.

Look, Miss Nobody's
rhyming! These days, she's
past curfew.

Ode to My Lost Glove

(January 23, 2019)

Forgive me, supple one,
I was too jittery

about reading poetry
to check my coat pockets.

Must have dropped you
darting to the Tennessee Theater.

What kind of beast
measures its life in words and pricey

second skins?
I pray icy fingers find you.

Today the overflow-homeless are sheltering in
Knoxville city buses.

Mine is a First World
problem. I'll vow

to be more careful,
more like Jane Hirshfield—

hold each object tenderly, like
Baby Buddha. Do not drop.

Recall minimum wage
at the Gimbel's scarf-and-glove counter?

Sang "Mr. Tambourine Man" on commuter trains,
echoing in tunnels.

Promised self I would stay in academia.
Stayed, and now I'm ranting for my city.

Treat every object like a glove
you'd cling to on a frigid night.

Treat every man better than
your first husband.

This one's a keeper.
Swear to lose less. If you must lose,

compose. Turn elegies
into odes.

Forgive me, husband,
for treating cash

off-handedly, as if I were Wilbur Ross on
a bad press day.

My new gloves from Bloomies boast
they were "hand-made,

in China." Forgive me, underpaid hands.
Thank you, noble Bobby D,

for twanging me through
department-store hell.

Treat a returning theme
like an old friend, new meaning.

1968, I sold handkerchiefs
under the cold eye

of my supervisor, Miss Freeburg.
Friends, it's a tissue world.

My little Buddha-glove
may be lying on the concrete floor

of Locust Street Parking, bargaining
with karma.

Its fist refused charity.
Lost chance, let my hands

become more giving.
Stray glove-sister,

may you be found by
some shivering soul

scurrying down Clinch,
down

South Gay
toward bright lights,

bold players,
buttery lobbies humming.

Whispering

At first I guessed
you were a petal in the
breeze, but it was

mid-May,
too late for
dogwoods. You

floated, fast
& light,
satin

moth. How I envy
your whisper over
ground! Some day

I will be lighter
o'er this earth—ancient
grammar—

in the
wind, as they
say.

NOTES

The epigraph from Paul Eluard is found in "Even When We
   Sleep," *Last Love Poems of Paul Eluard,* translated by
   Marilyn Kallet, Black Widow Press, 2006, pages 30–31.
   Eluard first published *"Même quand nous dormons,"* in
   Le dur désir de durer, 1946.

"Violins of Hope" is a project of concerts founded by Amnon
   Weinstein in 2012, using instruments rescued from the
   Holocaust. Conducted by Aram Demirjian, the Knoxville
   Symphony performed concerts with some of these treas-
   ured violins, Tennessee Theater, January 23–24, 2019.

My question in "Ode to a Lost Glove" echoes Adrienne Rich,
   "What kind of beast would turn its life into words?"
   The Dream of a Common Language: Poems 1974–1977,
   W.W. Norton & Company, 1978, 28.

MARILYN KALLET served two terms as Knoxville Poet Laureate, June 2018–June 2020. She has published 19 books, including *How Our Bodies Learned, The Love That Moves Me,* and *Packing Light: New and Selected Poems,* Black Widow Press. She translated Paul Eluard's *Last Love Poems* and Benjamin Péret's *The Big Game.* Dr. Kallet is Professor Emerita at the University of Tennessee. Since 2009, she has mentored poetry groups for the Virginia Center for the Creative Arts, in Auvillar, France. Her poems have appeared in *Plume, New Letters, Potomac Review, Still: The Journal,* and *American Diversity Report,* among others.

Contact: mkallet@utk.edu
Website: http://marilynkallet.com

BLACK WIDOW PRESS :: POETRY IN TRANSLATION